W9-DHX-903

Controlling
the Image

What's Inside

Notes to the Project Helper

This 4-H project book is designed for youth to explore and complete under the guidance of a project helper. This can be a parent, relative, project leader, friend, or knowledgeable adult. The duties of this individual begin with helping the child create and carry out a project plan. This is followed by helping the child Focus on each activity in his/her project plan, providing Support and Feedback for the learning taking place and conducting Debriefing sessions to determine what was done well, what could have been done differently, and where to go from here.

The information and activities contained in this book are arranged in a unique, experiential fashion (see model). In this way, youth are introduced to a particular practice, idea, or piece of information through an opening Photo Shoot (1) Experience. The results from the activity are then recorded in the accompanying pages. Following this, youth take the opportunity to (2) Share what they did with their Project Helper and (3) Process the experience through a series of questions allowing the learner to (4) Generalize, and (5) Apply the knowledge and skills gained. Project Helpers also provide encouragement for the learner to extend the experience by taking on one of the More Challenges provided at the end of each activity page.

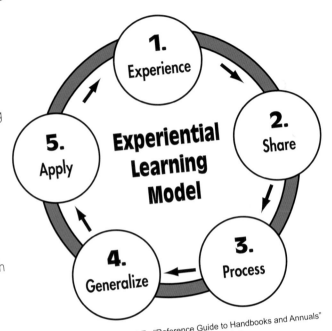

Pfeiffer, J.W., & Jones, J.E., "Reference Guide to Handbooks and Annuals"
© 1983 John Wiley & Sons, Inc.
Reprinted with permission of John Wiley & Sons, Inc.

Project Helper Expectations

- Review the Learner Outcomes (Photography Skill, Life Skill, Educational Standard and Success Indicator) on the lower left-hand side of each activity to understand the learning taking place. Each activity in this book is tied to a specific National Education Standard for Arts Education. See the inside back cover for a summary of these standards along with the goals and outcomes for this project.

- Become familiar with the Background sections and Photo Shoot activities contained in this book. The background information is intended to enlighten the Project Helper as much as the learner. Stay ahead of the learner by trying out activities beforehand. When noted on an activity page, check out the Fast Facts information on the 4-H Photo Kids web page.

- Begin the project by helping the learner establish his/her plan for the project. This is accomplished by reviewing and completing pages 3-7.

- Conduct a debriefing session allowing the learner to answer Review Questions and share results. This will improve their understanding about what was learned from an experiential perspective and the particular life skill and photography skill that were practiced.

- Use the Photo Journal as a discussion tool to help the learner celebrate what was done well and to see what could be done differently. Allow them to become better at assessing their own work.

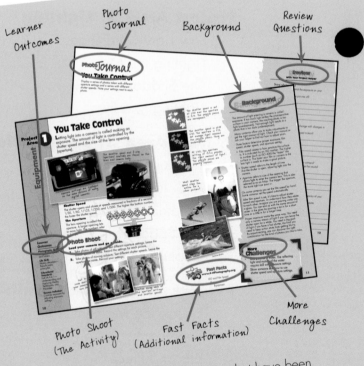

- Date and initial the activities that have been completed on page 4 of their project plan.

Fast Facts
www.4-HPhotography.org
Project Support

Project Planning Guide

Take Note

You will need access to an adjustable film-based or digital camera to complete this project.
See page 9 for more information.

This intermediate level project is designed for youth with prior experience in photography and those who have completed *Focus on Photography*, the first book in this series. It can be completed as a stand-alone project or in connection with another 4-H area of interest.

Check your county's project and record-keeping guidelines (if any) for additional requirements. This is especially important if you want to participate in county project judging or prepare an exhibit for competition. (See page 72 for details.) This project may be repeated if you select activities that were not satisfactorily completed or attempted in previous years. The More Challenges activities, which are optional, are a good source of additional activities if you choose to repeat this project. They may also inspire you to take a companion project or plan a self determined project on such topics as scrapbooking or photo editing.

Need some help getting started? Ask an adult or older youth photographer for ideas.

Your Project Guidelines

Complete the Planning Section of this Guide (Steps 1-4, pages 4-7).

Step 1—Explore each of the four Project Areas (Equipment, Lighting, Composition, and Skill Building) by completing all of the Photo Shoot activities in each area, along with the Photo Journal and Review sections.

As you complete your Photo Journal and Review Question pages, remember that they should reflect your best attempts to accomplish the activities. You can use the space any way you would like, including layering your photos to fit in the space provided. If you'd like more room for your photographs, remove the pages and put them into a three-ring binder. Add pages of your own or use the extra blank Photo Journal pages in the back of this book.

Step 2—Take part in at least two Organized Project Experiences.

Step 3—Become involved in at least two Leadership/Citizenship Activities.

Step 4—Take part in a Project Review.

Optional: More Challenges activities and the online Fast Facts are optional.

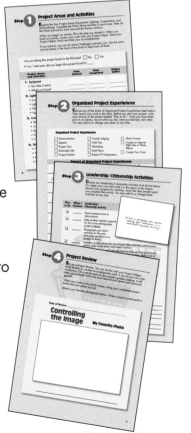

Project Areas and Activities

Explore the four Project Areas (Equipment, Lighting, Composition, and Skill Building). Complete the Photo Shoot activities in each area. Then do the Photo Journal (and the Review) for each one.

When you begin an activity, fill in the date you started it. When you finish an activity, review your work with your Project Helper. Have your Project Helper initial and date your accomplishment.

If you want to, you can do More Challenges activities, too. Use the extra journal sheets in the back of this book to keep track of those.

Are you taking this project book for the first time? ☐ Yes ☐ No

If "no," what year did you begin this project book?   20 _____

Project Areas and Activities	Date Started	Date Completed	Helper Initial
1. Equipment			
• You Take Control			
• What's in Focus?			
2. Lighting			
• Low Light Challenges			
• Lighting the Mood			
• The Shadows Show			
• Lighting in a Flash			
3. Composition			
• The Rule of Thirds			
• A Golden Photo			
• Building a Photo			
• The Space Tells a Story			
• Capture a Candid Photo			
4. Skill Building			
• Freeze the Moment			
• Panning the Action			
• Bits and Pieces			
• Panoramas			

Step 2 Organized Project Experiences

Choose two of the kinds of Organized Project Experiences listed below. Then record your work in the chart. Before you start your project, write your choices in the column labeled "Plan to Do." Once you have taken part in an activity, record what you did, what you learned, and when. You may add to or change your plans at any time.

Organized Project Experiences

- ☐ Demonstration
- ☐ Speech
- ☐ Project Tour
- ☐ Illustrated Talk
- ☐ Project Exhibit

- ☐ County Judging
- ☐ Field Trip
- ☐ Workshop
- ☐ Mall Show
- ☐ Radio/TV Presentation

- ☐ Short Course
- ☐ Create an Internet Web Site or Photo Album
- ☐ Create Your Own

Report of Organized Project Experiences

Plan to Do	What I Did	What I Learned	Date Completed
(Example) Demonstration	Showed club members how to create trick photography.	How fun it is to teach others about trick photograpy.	5/28

Step 3

Leadership/Citizenship Activities

Choose two Leadership/Citizenship activities from the list below, or create your own and write it in the space at the bottom. Record your progress by marking down the date (month/year) you complete the activity. You may add to or change these activities at any time.

(Attach a photograph with caption showing your involvement in a Leadership/Citizenship Activity.)

Plan to Do	When I Finished	Leadership/ Citizenship Activity
❑	_____	Teach someone how to take pictures.
❑	_____	Help another member prepare for his or her photography project judging.
❑	_____	Photograph your club's activities for the year and make an album or a display to share.
❑	_____	Volunteer to take photos for one of your other activities, such as your school, sports team, band, or choir.
❑	_____	Visit the local library and ask a librarian to help you find good books on photography. Display the books at a club meeting. Make a list of them for members to take home.
❑	_____	Help someone in your community organize his or her old photographs. Help them write down information about what the photographs show.
❑	_____	Have someone visit your club and talk about portrait, news, or sports photography.
❑	_____	Arrange for your club to tour a photo studio.
❑	_____	Have an experienced photographer visit your club and talk about portrait, news, or sports photography.
❑	_____	Arrange for your club to have a photo display in a public place.

Plan your own activities here:

❑	_____	_____
		_____
❑	_____	_____
		_____
❑	_____	_____

Project Review

Set up a Project Review. You can do this with your Project Helper, Club Leader, or another knowledgeable adult. It can be part of a club evaluation, or it can be part of your county's project judging. It will help you evaluate what you have learned and assess your personal growth.

When you come to the photo review, bring your completed project book and Photo Journal pages.

Attach your favorite photograph below. Write a caption underneath it.

Date of Review _____

Controlling the Image

My Favorite Photo

Introduction

Say cheese! Photography is all around us. It's in our homes and businesses, in magazines, and in schoolbooks. It's on television and on our favorite pages on the World Wide Web.

A photograph can tell a story. It can capture a friend's smile or international news. It can become a canvas on which we express ideas and emotion. It can be an interesting hobby and a rewarding job. You can become part of the fun by learning to use your camera in creative and effective ways that result in great pictures.

Good pictures *can* happen by accident. In order to take consistently great photographs, however, you have to learn how to control your image. You can do that by becoming more familiar with your camera's equipment and by mastering the techniques and tools used in composing a photograph. This project helps you do that.

Your camera equipment allows you to set aperture (f-stop), shutter speed, and more. These settings determine depth of field, focus, and exposure. When you know how to use these, you are able to create the effects you want with ease and consistency.

Controlling the Image also explores other components that affect a photograph, such as lighting (including flash) and picture composition. You will learn techniques to use in back light, low light, and silhouette shots. You will learn about the Rule of Thirds and the Golden Triangle. You will learn about viewpoints, positive and negative space, and taking candid photographs. All of these things help you set up interesting and aesthetically pleasing pictures and make your photographs look more and more professional.

Finally, you will bring together all the tools, techniques, and rules you have learned and begin "skill building." Skill building includes awesome techniques like panning, freezing the moment, and creating panoramas and montages.

To get the pictures on this page, a 4-H photographer used features on her camera to capture a stop-action photograph.

In each project area, you'll find an activity and these different sections.

- **Background** gives you details about what you are studying and tips for taking better pictures.

- **More Challenges** helps you grow as a photographer. It allows you to practice and expand on what you just learned.

- **Photo Journal** pages allow you to display your work near the project. (You can remove these pages and put them in a three-ring binder if you need more room or want to add pages of your own.) You'll be able to study your results and share them with your friends and family. You'll see your pictures become better and better as your technique and your talent grow!

Photo by Carl Wulff, 4-H Youth Photographer

Freeze the moment!

Have fun with this project! Let this book be your guide as you master your camera's equipment and photo techniques. Express yourself through pictures. Let the pictures in this book spark your imagination, and then move on to create your own work of art. Remember, control your image and take better pictures!

What You Need

The better you get to know your camera, the better prepared you are to take great pictures! You don't have to have a fancy camera to take good pictures. A good eye and a good imagination are much more important. But you do need more than a "point and shoot" camera to do the activities in this project. You need to have access to a film or digital camera with a flash and adjustable settings.

Once you have a camera, study it. Find and check off these camera parts. See how many of them your camera has.

☐ Body ☐ Lens ☐ Shutter ☐ Release button
☐ On/off button ☐ Viewfinder ☐ Video screen
☐ Built-in flash ☐ Battery compartment

Find out if your camera has a "manual" mode. You need to be able to change its shutter speed, film speed, and aperture. Read the owner's manual. Get tips from someone who knows about that kind of camera. Get your camera ready to take pictures. Get film or make room on the memory card, and make sure you have fresh batteries.

It is also very helpful to have access to a tripod and to a separate flash (one not built in to your camera). If you don't, see if someone else has them and is willing to share.

This symbol tells you how to find more information at the 4-H Photo Kids Project Online site, www.4-HPhotography.org. Check it out!

Fast Facts
www.4-HPhotography.org

You Take Control

Letting light into a camera is called making an exposure. The amount of light is controlled by the shutter speed and the size of the lens opening (aperture).

Exposure settings are displayed on the video screens of many digital cameras.

The shutter speed and f-stop (aperture) controls are found on the lens and camera body.

Shutter Speed

The shutter opens and closes at speeds measured in fractions of a second: 1/30, 1/60, 1/125, 1/250, and 1/500. The higher the bottom number, the faster the shutter speed.

The Aperture

The lens opening is called the aperture. A larger opening lets in more light. The numbers refer to f-stops.

f/ 22   f/ 16   f/ 11   f/ 8   f/ 5.6   f/ 4   f/ 2.8

Photo Shoot

Load your camera and go outside.

1. Take photos of still subjects. Test different aperture settings. Leave the shutter speed the same. Record the settings for each picture.

2. Take photos of moving subjects. Test different shutter speeds. Leave the aperture the same. Record your settings.

Learner Outcomes

Photography Skill:
Using shutter speeds and f-stops

Life Skill:
Makes decisions—Recalls basic principles

Educational Standard:
NA-VA.K-4.1—Understanding and Applying Media, Techniques, and Processes

Success Indicator:
Controls exposure by adjusting exposure settings

Get to know what your camera can do.

Practice using each of the aperture settings and shutter speeds.

Photo by Katie Pflueger, 4-H Youth Photographer

The shutter speed is set at 1/60 and the aperture is f/4. The puzzle pieces are overexposed.

The shutter speed is still 1/60. The aperture is f/11. Not enough light reached the puzzle pieces. They are underexposed.

At 1/60, the aperture setting of f/5.6 provides the right amount of light. The puzzle pieces are properly exposed.

What shutter speed stops the motion for a clear picture?

Archive photos

The amount of light entering a camera is called exposure. If too much light strikes the photosensitive surface in your camera, the resulting photo is too light (overexposed). Not enough light results in a photo that is too dark (underexposed).

Many cameras allow you to make adjustments to get the right amount of light. Check your manual or ask your helper to find out how to adjust yours.

Three factors determine proper exposure: film speed, shutter speed, and aperture setting.

- Film speed relates to how sensitive the surface is. It is indicated by an ISO number. The higher its number (such as ISO 400) the "faster" the surface is. The faster your film or camera is the less light it needs to make a good picture.

- Shutter speed refers to the length of time that the shutter is open, allowing light into the camera.

- Aperture refers to size of the opening that allows light to enter the camera lens. This is also referred to as an f-stop. The bigger the aperture, the more light can pour in.

On some cameras you set the film speed by hand. Some cameras set the speed automatically.

After film speed is set, it's time to adjust shutter speed and aperture. To understand how they relate to each other, imagine you are pouring water into a glass. You can end up with the same amount of water in the glass by pouring a lot in for a short time or a little in for a longer time.

Proper exposure works the same way. You need only a narrow stream of light if you can leave the shutter open for a while. You need a big gush of light if you have a fast shutter, the kind you need to keep action shots from getting blurry. By experimenting, you can discover the right combination for the kind of photos you like to take.

More Challenges

- Take pictures of water. The reflecting light and motion of the water require skill with exposure settings.
- Show someone else how to use shutter speed and aperture settings.

Photo Journal
You Take Control

Display a series of photos taken with different aperture settings and a series with different shutter speeds. Note your settings next to each photo.

Share what you did
- How did you control the exposure on your camera?
- What did you take pictures of?

_____

_____

_____

_____

Process
- How did your pictures change with changes in the aperture?
- What shutter speed stopped motion?

_____

_____

_____

_____

Generalize
- What is happening inside the camera?
- How do the mechanics change the results?

_____

_____

_____

_____

Apply
- How does understanding the mechanics of your camera help?
- What other activities and careers require understanding equipment?

_____

_____

_____

Equipment

What's in Focus?

Aperture settings determine what is in focus. The area of sharp focus is the depth of field.

The foreground is sharp but the background is blurry. The depth of field is shallow. The aperture was set at f/2. Larger apertures (openings) keep less area in sharp focus.

The foreground and background are sharp. The depth of field is deeper. The aperture is set at f/8. Smaller apertures (openings) keep more of your picture in focus.

Learner Outcomes

Photography Skill:
Adjusting the depth of field

Life Skill:
Acquiring and evaluating information—Obtains information and validates outcomes

Educational Standard:
NA-VA.K-4.1—Understanding and Applying Media, Techniques, and Processes

Success Indicator:
Uses aperture settings to control the depth of field

Photo Shoot

Select a daylight scene.

1. **Picture 1**—Set the aperture at its largest opening (f/2.8 to f/4). Adjust the shutter speed to get the right exposure.

2. **Picture 2**—Set the aperture at its smallest opening (f/8 to f/22, depending on your camera). Adjust the shutter speed.

3. Compare the depth of field in Picture #1 and Picture #2.

Background

Tips

Small f-stop numbers give you a small depth of field (limited focus). Larger f-stop numbers give you larger depth of field (everything in focus).

The term used to describe how much of a scene is in focus is "depth of field." If the depth of field in your photograph is "deep," objects in front of and behind your focal point are in focus, too. If the depth of field is "shallow," those objects are blurry.

Aperture settings, or f-stops, can help you control what is in focus and what is out of focus in a scene. In order to use them, though, you have to remember to think in opposites. That's because the larger an f-stop number, the smaller the lens opening. And the smaller the opening, the greater the depth of field.

- Small f-stop number (like f/5.6) = large opening = shallow depth of field
- Large f-stop number (like f/11) = small opening = deep depth of field

Depth of field is a great creative tool when you are shooting certain kinds of photos. For example, if you want to shoot a portrait and make the background blurry, select a smaller f-stop. If the background is important and you want it in focus, select a higher f-stop.

Keeping track of your exposure is important when you are learning this technique. Carry a small notebook and pen or pencil with you. Your digital camera may record the exposure setting for each photo you take.

Photo by Doyle Gates, 4-H Photo Volunteer

No doubt this close-up shot with blurred background is using a smaller F-stop.

Photo by Jeff Vogtschaller, 4-H Photo Volunteer

This chess set was taken at F-11. See how the foreground and background stay in focus.

More Challenges

- Search magazines and newspapers for pictures with a shallow depth of field. Notice how professionals use depth of field.
- Shutter speed, aperture, and film speed are interrelated. Discover how ISO settings impact the depth of field. Take pictures using different ISO settings or rolls of film with different film speeds.

Photo Journal
What's in Focus?

Take three sets of pictures, each set with a different subject. Shoot them at different apertures. Post them here and compare the depth of field results.

Review
with Your Project Helper

Share what you did
- How did you change the aperture settings on your camera?
- How did the depth of field change?

_____

_____

_____

Process
- Why would you want to put a certain part of a picture out of focus?
- How does depth of field change the way you feel about a picture?

_____

_____

Generalize
- How might wedding photographers use depth of field?
- Where else have you seen photographs that use a shallow depth of field?

_____

_____

Apply
- One way to remember how depth of field works is to think "The smaller the f-stop, the smaller the area in focus." What are some other devices you use to remember things?
- What other things do people do where writing down details is helpful?

_____

_____

Low Light Challenges

Weather conditions and the time of day change the natural light. Adjust your settings for interesting pictures in natural low light.

Photo by Barb Lassa,
4-H Photo Volunteer

This early morning shot of sheep standing in the mist is just as striking as this late evening shot at a boat dock.

Learner Outcomes

Photography Skill:
Adjusts aperture and shutter speed for natural low light

Life Skill:
Making decisions—Applies principles to the situation

Educational Standard:
NA-VA.K-4.1—Understanding and Applying Media, Techniques, and Processes

Success Indicator:
Takes pictures in natural low light

Photo Shoot

1. **Dawn**—Capture the orange glow and the long shadows as the sun rises.

2. **Sunset**—Best when the sun is about to touch the horizon. Add a person for interest. Your shutter speed should be slow.

3. **Dusk**—15 to 30 minutes after sunset. Shoot from one end of a fence or looking down a road. A tripod is necessary.

4. **Bad weather**—Heavy rain, fog, and clouds add mystery and drama. Try one f-stop less than indicated for emphasis.

Tips

For sharp pictures in low light

- Larger lens openings (small f-stops) have less depth of field. Focus carefully.

- Slower shutter speeds can blur motion. Keep things steady.

- High ISO/fast film is better for stopping action.

Painting with light. You will need a totally dark area, a camera on a tripod, and someone with a flashlight.

This is a long exposure taken of fireworks.

Photo by Elizabeth Scarpitti, 4-H Youth Photographer

Photo by Collin Hall, 4-H Youth Photographer

This is a long exposure taken of speeding cars on the freeway.

Imagine taking pictures of fireworks or the lights of a city at night. Low-light situations such as these present a number of challenges. If you can overcome them, though, the results can be awesome!

There are certain things to keep in mind when photographing low-light scenes.

- First of all, if your camera has a built-in meter you can't always rely on it. The light can be too weak for the meter to work right. You'll have to experiment with exposure settings in order to find one that records the scene accurately.

- Second, you need a tripod. Because shutter speeds have to be slow in order to gather in enough light, the camera has to stay perfectly still. Otherwise, your shots will be blurry.

- Always turn off your flash when shooting in low light. The flash is useless for far away scenes and often ruins the effect of what you are shooting.

- Use a fast film or set your digital camera to a high film speed such as ISO 400. This makes the camera more sensitive to light and allows you to use higher f-stops and faster shutter speeds.

- Finally, see if your camera has a "B" setting that lets you hold the shutter open for as long as you want—for seconds or even minutes. Experiment with very different exposures. Be sure to write the times down, so you can see which ones worked the best.

More Challenges

- Take some pictures in snow. Give a slight overexposure (slower shutter speed) to keep white snow looking whiter.

- Take pictures at night of a downtown street. Turn off your flash. Don't let the built-in exposure meter confuse you; it sees too much darkness.

- Try some long exposures in the dark. With "B," the shutter stays open as long as you hold the shutter release down. You'll need a tripod.

Fast Facts

www.4-HPhotography.org

Long Exposures and Painting with Light

PhotoJournal
Low Light
Challenges

Display your favorite "low light" pictures. Write down the speeds and lens openings you used.

Share what you did
- What situations did you photograph?
- How did you adjust your camera?

_____

_____

_____

Process
- What did you like about your results?
- How did your photos capture the mood?

_____

_____

Generalize
- What kind of challenges can occur in bad weather?
- What should you do to be safe when you are working in low light conditions?

_____

_____

_____

Apply
- Which professional photographers have to use natural low light techniques in their work?
- Do most jobs have challenges to overcome? What kinds of special techniques do family members and friends have to know to do their jobs well?

_____

_____

Lighting the Mood

Pictures create moods and communicate feelings. Strong sunlight produces hard, bright contrasting highlights. Clouds and shade produce diffused light with soft shadows. You can use hard light and soft light to communicate feelings.

Strong sunlight produces hard details, with bright highlights and dark shadows...

...while subdued sunlight tends to soften shades and blend shadows.

Photo by Doyle Gates, 4-H Photo Volunteer

Learner Outcomes

Photography Skill:
Capturing hard and soft light to create moods

Life Skill:
Communicating with others—Communicates non-verbal messages

Educational Standard:
NA-VA.K-4.1—Understanding and Applying Media, Techniques, and Processes

Success Indicator:
Communicates feelings through hard and soft light in photos

Photo Shoot

Take photos for hard light and soft light results. Compare hard light from mid-day and soft light from pre-dawn or early morning hours. Choose from these subjects.

- lakes, rivers, or landscapes
- buildings, monuments
- people or still life
- close-ups for detail

Photo by Doyle Gates, 4-H Photo Volunteer

The soft light and warm color from the sunset create a calm and peaceful mood.

Photo by Shirley Gates, 4-H Photo Volunteer

Very soft shadows were created by diffused light.

Many things determine what makes a great photo. You have learned that the colors, shadows, and textures in your photo depend on the kind of light you have—whether it is hard or soft. The quality of light in a scene can also affect how the viewer *feels* about your photograph. Lighting and mood can be just as important as technical aspects.

How do photographers use light quality to suggest mood? There are many ways. For example, a cloudy, foggy day can show a dreary mood much better than a bright sunny one. Midday sunshine can create a lively mood for sports and outdoor action photos. The long shadows and warm colors created by a setting sun can suggest a mellow or sad mood.

Don't let bad weather keep you from going outside and taking pictures. Get in the habit of making the most of whatever kind of weather you have—it can help you create the mood you want. Some of the most famous photos ever shot were taken when the weather was less than perfect!

More Challenges

- Make a friend look powerful. Choose a camera angle and hard lighting for the portrait.

- Show texture in sharp detail and flat detail. Try close-ups using rough, smooth, and shiny surfaces. Experiment with hard and soft light for best results.

- At the end of a day, when shadows are at their longest, photograph a subject or scene that gives a feeling of loneliness, isolation, or sadness.

Fast Facts
www.4-HPhotography.org

Advance the Sunset

Photo Journal
Lighting the Mood

Choose two photos that illustrate hard light
and two photos that illustrate soft light.
Describe the moods you captured.

Photo of a statue lit only from a northern window.

The subject with window light from the right and light reflected into the shadow area. White cardboard makes a good reflector.

The flash was diffused with layers of masking tape. Light passing through the tape gives the subject golden warmth.

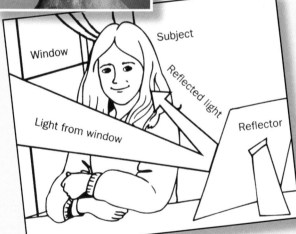

Photographers work with both natural (sun-produced) light and artificial light (the kind produced by room lights and the flashes on their cameras). They also work with the way that light falls on their subjects—whether it is direct, reflected, or diffused.

What do these terms mean? Again, it may help to think of the light in your photo as a stream of water.

- **Direct light** is like the water coming out of a hose full blast. Direct light is very strong. It results in very clean details, but it produces harsh shadows.

- **Reflected light** is like water that bounces off a wall after coming out of the hose. It washes the scene with light, but the light is not as hard. It creates crisp details, but it has softer shadows.

- **Diffused light** is found outdoors on an overcast day or in deep shade. It is like the water that comes out of a sprinkler. It showers the scene with the softest light of all, painting soft details and shadows.

You should remember this when you use the flash on your camera. Using direct flash gives you lots of detail, but if you're taking pictures of people, that big splash of light can cause them to scrunch their eyes shut or look uncomfortable. To avoid this, use reflected or diffused light. If you can aim your flash, point it at the ceiling or walls to bounce light back on your subject. (That's what professional photographers are doing when they use umbrellas to reflect light from studio flash units.) Diffuse the impact of the light from your flash by covering it with white cloth or tracing paper.

More Challenges

- Set your flash on manual for close-up work. (This works best with a separate flash.)
  —Fasten four lens-cleaning tissues around the flash head with a rubber band.
  —Hold the flash 15 inches from the subject. Take flash pictures at f/8, f/11, and f/16. If they are underexposed or overexposed add or remove lens tissues.
- Build a reflector and a diffuser to bounce and soften natural light.

Photo Journal

Lighting in a Flash

Post your favorite flash photos. Record what you did to get results.

Using these three rules can produce a balance in a variety of photos.

Rule of Thirds

Photo by Doyle Gates, 4-H Photo Volunteer

Golden Triangle

Golden Rectangle

Place the focal point off-center in your viewfinder. Sometimes this can make your photo look awkward. Sometimes, though, it can give your photo extra life.

Are you ready to explore new ways to compose pictures? Try one of the three "rules" invented to help make off-center composition work well: The Rule of Thirds, The Golden Triangle, and the Golden Rectangle.

These rules have something in common: They help draw the viewer's eyes through the composition. They do this with repeated elements, patterns, and specific placement of lines and shapes.

These basic rules are called design principles. They have been around for centuries! Remember: Photography is a form of art, like drawing and painting. It may seem easier to create art through photography, but the rules that work for other art forms also apply to photography.

Find a book or a museum website that has paintings from many different centuries and many different cultures, from Botticelli to Picasso and from Africa to Asia. Can you find examples of the three rules of composition you have just learned? Look at how paintings, drawings, and prints make use of color, texture, and pattern. What else can these kinds of art teach you about how to compose your photographs? These lessons can mean the difference between taking snapshots and creating art!

More Challenges

- Share your photos with a professional photographer. Take notes on how to improve your skills.
- Take some creative photos that look like art. Ask others for their opinions.

Photo Journal

Golden Photo

Display a photo using the Rule of Thirds, one using the Golden Triangle, one using the Golden Rectangle—and one that you like that doesn't follow the rules. Label each one.

Review
with Your Project Helper

Share what you did
- Which template was the most difficult to make and why?
- Share your photos showing each of the three rules.

_____

_____

_____

Process
- Which photo do you like the best and why?
- Which photo rule was the most difficult to use? Why?

_____

_____

_____

Generalize
- Share a good photo that does not follow the rules. Why do you like it?
- What would happen if every photo followed the composition rules exactly? Would the results be appealing? Would they be artistic?

_____

_____

_____

Apply
- General "rules of thumb" can be very helpful. Name some that have helped you in other activities.
- Do you think that design principles are the same in every culture in every part of the world? Why or why not?

_____

_____

_____

Building a Photo

Explore your world! Photograph familiar places and people. Try different viewpoints on the same subject.

How can you make this photo of President Lincoln more interesting?

Lincoln's face is framed by his right arm, leg, and chest.

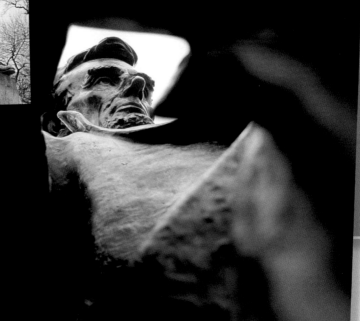

Learner Outcomes

Photography Skill:
Using different viewpoints to create better photos

Life Skill:
Thinking creatively—Actively pursues creative expression

Educational Standard:
NA-VA.K-4.3—Choosing and Evaluating a Range of Subject Matter, Symbols, and Ideas

Success Indicator:
Takes photos using different viewpoints

Photo Shoot

Choose a familiar subject and take photos. Ask yourself the questions below. Then move the camera or move yourself!

1. Vertical or horizontal?

2. Stand up, crouch down, or get up high?

3. Far away or close up?

4. Rule of Thirds? Try the focal point in different places.

5. Check for clutter?

6. Perspective? Do you need something in the photo to show the real size of the subject?

Review
with Your Project Helper

Share what you did

- Point to the positive and negative space in three photos.
- Choose one photo and tell the story that you were trying to create.

Process

- Which of your photos is your favorite and why?
- What is difficult about capturing a story in one picture?

Generalize

- How can backgrounds improve photos of events like graduations and parties?
- How can backgrounds ruin a good photo?

Apply

- A portrait photographer looks at a background differently than a photojournalist. Why?
- Give titles or captions to each of your photos that help to tell the story or inform people.

Composition

Capture a Candid Photo

Candid photography captures moments that are unposed. Candid photos are taken at birthday parties, sports games, and other events.

Candid photos are everywhere. In a parking lot, living room, and even a museum.

Photo by Stephanie Koenig, 4-H Youth Photographer

Photo by Jena Richards, 4-H Youth Photographer

Learner Outcomes

Photography Skill:
Taking candid photographs to capture a moment in time

Life Skill:
Thinking creatively—Actively pursues creative expression

Educational Standard:
NA-VA.5-8.3—Choosing and Evaluating a Range of Subject Matter, Symbols, and Ideas

Success Indicator:
Takes candid photos

Photo Shoot

Create a Candid Collection. Take photographs at a party, parade, family reunion, or sporting event.

- Capture the emotion of the event. Do the people show the same facial expressions?

- Capture people all doing the same thing: cheering, playing, swimming, or dancing. Action shots require planning ahead. Watch for the moment when there is a change and the movement slows down slightly.

- Try babies and children. Be ready and take your photos quickly. Babies and children are not very patient.

Share what you did

- What bits and pieces did you photograph?
- What changes did you make in your camera settings?

_____

_____

Process

- What do you like about each photograph you took?
- What was difficult about looking for interesting close-ups?

_____

_____

_____

Generalize

- What practical use do close-up photos have?
- How can bits and pieces be used to create photography as art?

_____

_____

_____

Apply

- How has this experience taught you to look at things differently?
- What are some other times when it is important to focus on details?

_____

_____

_____

Panoramas

Don't be frustrated by how little the camera can see of a huge landscape. Take a series of pictures from the same spot and put them together.

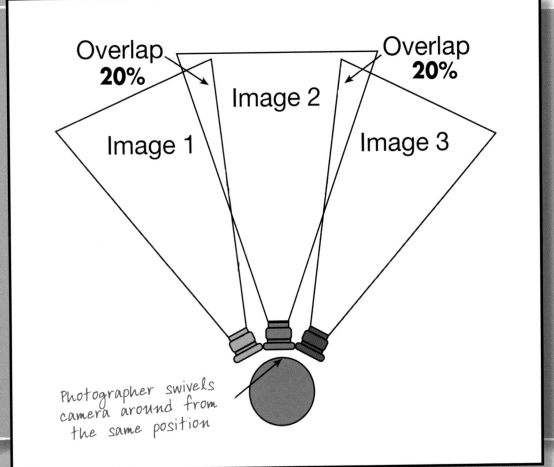

Overlap **20%**

Overlap **20%**

Image 1 Image 2 Image 3

Photographer swivels camera around from the same position

Photo Shoot

1. Choose a panoramic scene. Decide on the features you want to include and take several photos from the same spot.

2. Find a level surface such as a wall or post to support your camera. Use a tripod to keep it steady and level.

3. Position the camera to take the first shot. Then swivel the camera to the next part of the scene. Include a 20% overlap. It will help when you put the prints together. You can take three angles or reposition your camera around a full 360° to get a complete circle.

Tips For Youth Photo Exhibitors

- Be extremely neat when mounting your photos. Follow specifications for correct size of photos and color of mounting boards, mounting glue, and other mounting materials. (Hint: Rubber cement works well for temporary mounting at county fairs. It also is easy to clean up. Never use photo or art corners for mounting, even if they're not forbidden in the fair book.) Present a clean, neat exhibit with all cement and pencil marks removed.

- Follow good layout rules for a photo exhibit. That means no extra artwork on the mounting board such as curlicues, drawings, arrows, or balloons for quotes. Never mount your photos at an angle or on a slant. Judges want photos set squarely and neatly on the mounting board. If titles and captions are required, spell the words correctly, use proper grammar, and don't use cliché or overused phrases. If titles and captions are not required, neatly number the photos, left to right and top to bottom — the way we read a page. If cropping is allowed, crop photos either to a square or a rectangle, not a circle, triangle, or other odd shape.

- Provide technical information about your photos such as the camera used, type of film, type of lighting, exposure details, etc. Attaching a 3"x 5" card with this information to the back of your exhibit works well. If this technical information is not required at your county fair, assume that the judge will ask for it during face-to-face or conference judging. Be prepared. Having the information somewhere on the board saves time for judges and also gets you in the habit of recording this vital information.

- Don't worry about the type of camera you use for your photos. Any camera will do. Judges are being encouraged to judge each photo primarily on the basis of its composition and story-telling ability. You can take interesting, well-composed photographs with any camera. You can compete with someone using much more expensive equipment as long as you submit photos that follow the rules of composition and that tell a story.

By Wayne Brabender, Wisconsin 4-H Photography Specialist

What's Next?

You may think you're finished now, but if you are interested in photography there is much more to do. You can:

- Build on the lessons you learned about exhibiting photographs. Help your family mat, frame, and display its favorite pictures.

- Take and frame photos to give to special people for their birthdays, anniversaries, or holidays.

- Keep a scrapbook of photos that you like. You can use it when you need ideas.

- Do research on jobs that use photography and the kinds of education, training, and experience you need to do them.

Be sure to check out the final 4-H Photo Kids project book, *Mastering Photography*. It will teach you more exciting techniques and prepare you to put together an attractive and interesting portfolio that you can use to look for photography work or to apply to an art program.

Want to share your work with more people? Submit your photos to the National 4-H Photo contest. Use this link to find more information.

Fast Facts
www.4-HPhotography.org

National 4-H Photo Contest

www.4-HPhotography.org

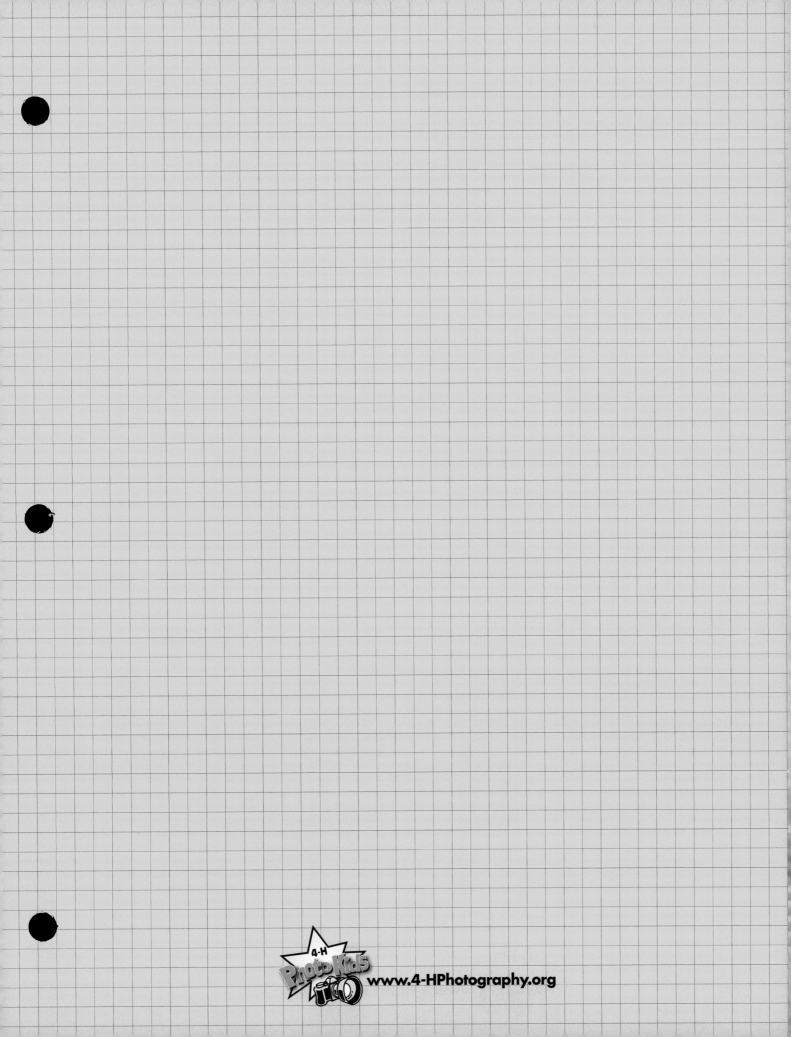